DOVER'S TRAMWAYS

Robert J Harley

MP Middleton Press

First published November 1993

ISBN 1 873793 24 3

© Middleton Press 1993

Design - Deborah Goodridge

Published by Middleton Press
            Easebourne Lane
            Midhurst
            West Sussex
            GU29 9AZ
            Tel: (0730) 813169
(From 16 April 1995 - (01730) 813169)

Printed & bound by Biddles Ltd,
            Guildford and Kings Lynn

CONTENTS

INTRODUCTION AND ACKNOWLEDGEMENTS

At the age of twelve, I received a copy of J.V.Horn's book on Dover Corporation Tramways as a Christmas present; from the very first page a fascinating story emerged. The work has rightly become a classic on small town tramway operation in Great Britain. My interest in Dover and its tramways was fired; this was the inspiration for the present volume. I would like to thank the photographers and enthusiasts who have made it all possible: C.Carter, M.J.O'Connor, R.Elliott, G.L.Gundry, R.Hollingsbee, D.C.Padgham, I.Gotheridge, D.Collyer and G.N.Southerden. J.S.Webb and Stan Letts from the West Midlands have also helped with information and photographs. A special vote of thanks goes to Rosy Thacker and Glyn Wilton of the library at the National Tramway Museum for all their help in unearthing scarce material. Pam and Bill Price of East Grinstead also deserve a mention, for they were the donors of that original Christmas present, little did they then realise that their nephew would go on to author

a series of tramway books. The dimensions of some of the car plans which appear in the Rolling Stock section have been taken from original work by P.Hammond and W.Gratwicke and I am very grateful for the assistance.

Finally, I must pay tribute to J.G.Harman without whose guidance this work would have been a lot poorer; Joe was a conductor on the tramways and he had the foresight to carry a camera with him. All students of local history owe him a debt of gratitude and the results of his work can be seen in the following pages. He has been very patient in answering many questions about the system; I hope he forgives me for all the phone calls! I would like to dedicate this latest volume in the Tramway Classics series to Joe and all his colleagues, the men and women who kept Dover Corporation Tramways in operation during many lean and uncertain years; their public service was unmatched.

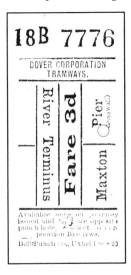

GEOGRAPHICAL SETTING

The town of Dover in the county of Kent is situated along the valley of the River Dour which flows into the Channel. At the estuary of the river a port was established. The land rises steeply from the valley to the North Downs. These are chalk hills which end at the seashore in the world famous white cliffs formation.

The Ordnance Survey maps are to the scale of 25" to 1 mile and from the 3rd edition on 1907.

HISTORICAL BACKGROUND

This area has been known for many centuries as the "Gateway to England." As a centre of coastal trade and the premier Cinque Port it has seen much activity and Dover has always had a strategic significance in the defence of the realm due to its proximity to the continent. The fine castle guarding the town reminds us of this role. A railway connection to the capital opened via the neighbouring port of Folkestone in 1844 and a direct line to Canterbury and London was completed in 1861. The two railways brought much cross-channel traffic and a commercial harbour was constructed for continental bound shipping. Unlike many other south coast towns, Dover has never developed into a tourist resort, and most visitors pass through the town en route to the ferry port.

An electric tramway system was opened in 1897, making Dover one of the country's pioneers in this form of traction. The main line extended from Buckland to the harbour at Clarence Place and came into use on 6th September 1897. A branch ran along Folkestone Road to terminate at Maxton and carried traffic from December of that year. Depots were provided at both Buckland and Maxton. The track gauge was 3ft 6ins/1067mm and the original fleet consisted of eight trams and two trailer cars.

The tramways always served a natural traffic route and their success was guaranteed. The village of River was joined to the main line in 1905 by a cross country route that included private right of way through fields. The town's tramways were isolated from other systems, although there were proposals for lines to St. Margarets and Martin Mill. A serious accident on Crabble Road in 1917 resulted in a recommendation from the inspecting officer that no passengers be permitted on the top decks of cars travelling along Crabble Hill to River. Overcrowding of cars was also a problem during World War I. The system settled down and it was blessed with a devoted staff who toiled through the financially insecure times of the 1920s to keep the fleet running. Dover became famous amongst the tramway fraternity for the purchase of second hand rolling stock, which prolonged the life of the system, and the town was known for the many different types of tramcar in a variety of liveries! This colourful situation could not last and the council concluded an agreement with the East Kent Roadcar Company for the replacement of trams by buses. Electric traction ceased on the streets of Dover on the last day of 1936, and the trams were subsequently broken up.

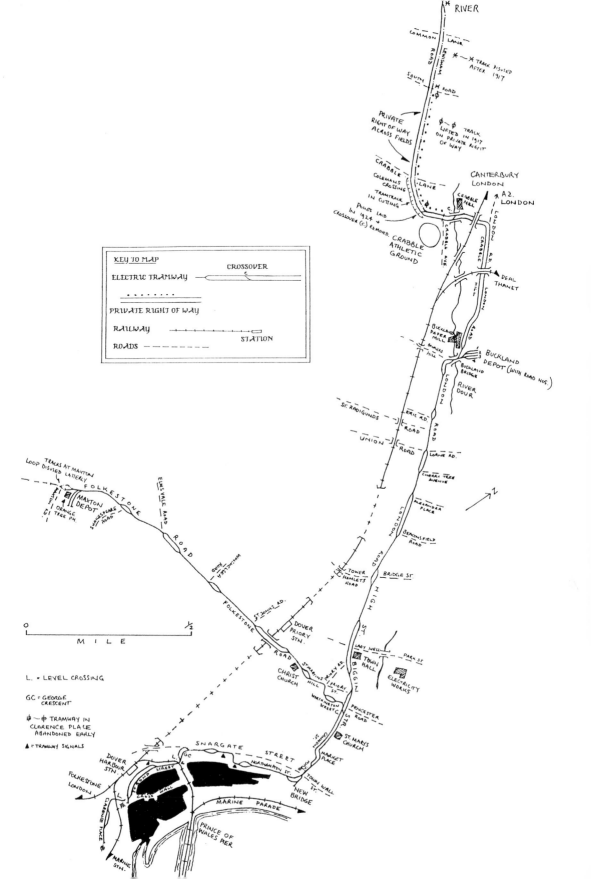

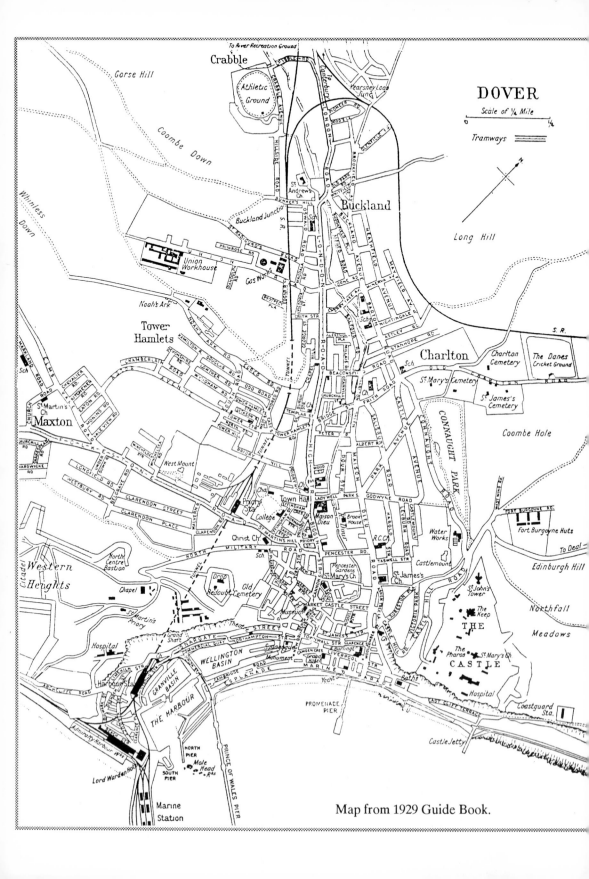

Map from 1929 Guide Book.

1. Main Line

1. We start our tour of Dover at the small Kentish village of River, little more than a hamlet when the trams arrived in 1905. The end of the track is clearly visible as a proud motorman poses at the controls of the green and cream tramcar. (R.J.Harley Coll.)

2. A winter scene at River terminus with driver Harry Brett and conductor P.W. Harman, the father of J.G.Harman who continued the family tradition of working on the tramways. (J.G.Harman)

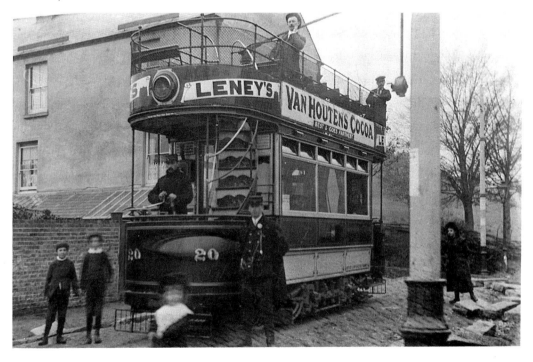

3.   Car 22 was purchased from Birmingham Corporation in 1933. It is seen here in blue livery and was photographed in the mid 1930s by Joe Harman just before he climbed aboard to signal the departure.   (J.G.Harman)

4. A sunny day in 1935 and car 4, one of the second hand buys from West Hartlepool in 1927, glistens in its deep red and cream colours. (B.R.Miller)

5. A study in light and shade as car 27 waits to leave. From the shadow on the opposite wall it seems that the conductor is engaged in an armed hold-up of top deck passengers! Perhaps in this summer 1922 view, he has been reading too many accounts of contemporary events in American cities. (G.L.Gundry)

These Bye-Laws and Regulations shall come in force on the First day of November, 1897.

No passenger shall smoke inside any car or on either platform.

No passenger or other person shall, while travelling in or upon any car, play or perform upon any musical instrument.

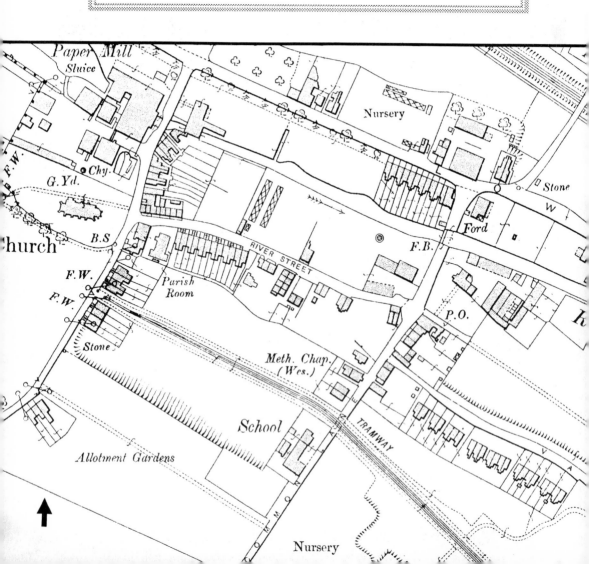

6. Car 17, the only member of the fleet with reversed stairs, stands on the original double track which stretches towards town. Note the very rough state of the roadway in this view which was taken in October 1905, shortly after opening of the River section. The Methodist chapel on Common Lane is seen behind the tram. (J.G.Harman Coll.)

7. In Lewisham Road the track on the eastern side had been disused since 1917, hence this view of car 4 about to proceed to Dover on the wrong side of the road. However, in those days there was very little other traffic to worry about. (National Tramway Museum)

8. Looking north along Lewisham Road in 1936 and car 22 has the thoroughfare to itself. (J.G.Harman)

9. Summer 1922 and the last of the houses is reached before the tramway traverses open country. (G.L.Gundry)

10. At the same spot as the previous photo; the date is now July 1934 and some of the famous British semi-detached houses are beginning to encroach on the rural aspect. The notice warns against trespassing on the tramway and the remains of the second track on the road crossing can be seen. (G.N.Southerden)

11. You can almost feel the warm sun in this tramway idyll as car 22 heads for town. This rural excursion was very popular with ramblers and summer Sundays saw plenty of passengers using the tram to River on their way to explore the scenery of the Alkham Valley. (B.R.Miller)

12. Just beyond Coleman's Crossing a line of cars waits for the scrapman in this January 1937 picture. Buses had already taken over from the trams and the River reserved track was selected as the final resting place for these open top cars. After the sledgehammer and the breaker's torch had done their work, the track was removed and the right of way made up as an extension of Lewisham Road. (National Tramway Museum)

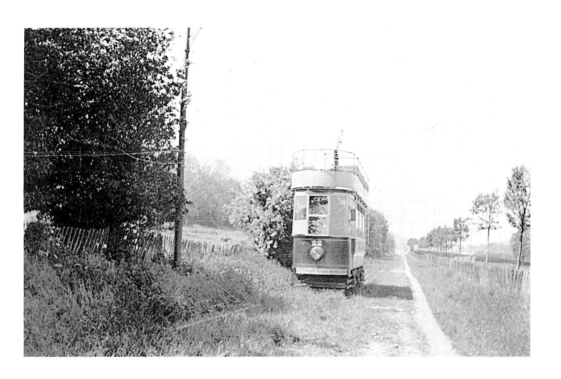

13. Car 22 approaches Coleman's Crossing. The gentle sweep of the downland countryside can be glimpsed to the left of the tram. Occasionally the tram would stop here to cater for visitors to St.Radigund's Abbey and for a couple of minutes the top deck passengers would often be treated to the sound and sight of skylarks rising from the fields. (G.N.Southerden)

14. The pole behind car 22, where the lady is standing, marks the end of the reserved track. Double track then led all the way past the Crabble Athletic Ground to Buckland Depot. (I.Gotheridge Coll.)

15. Newly delivered car 19 pauses in front of Crabble Athletic Ground. Note the splendid condition of this tram built in 1905. Sports fixtures at this location included the annual visit of the Kent County Cricket Club to play two first class matches during Cricket Week every August. (D.C.Padgham Coll.)

16. At around 3.25 on the afternoon of 19th August 1917, car 20 with Driver Bissenden at the controls got into trouble descending Crabble Hill. The tram gained speed, left the rails and crashed into the wall of the Crabble Paper Mill seen here. (R.J.Harley Coll.)

17. The wreckage tells a sorry tale of death and destruction. Amongst the ten fatalities was the young conductress Lottie Scrase; 59 passengers were injured, many seriously. The official accident report relates..."a soldier (Trooper Gunner) and a gentleman (Naval Pensioner Miller) went on the platform after the driver had jumped off. It is not clear whether these men attempted to work the brakes or not....In any case, no retardation of speed was effected." (R.J.Harley Coll.)

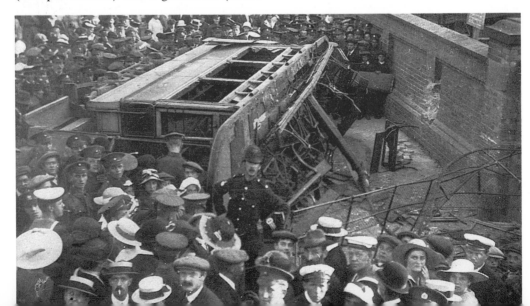

18. Like a beached whale, car 20 lies stranded across the roadway. Colonel Pringle who conducted the official enquiry lays the blame squarely on the unfortunate Bissenden; one suspects that it might have been better for the motorman if he had stayed at his post and "gone down with his ship!" The feeling amongst some of the tram crews was that the manager, E.C.Carden, was at least partly responsible on account of poor judgement and inadequate supervision of trainee motormen. (R.J.Harley Coll.)

19. Car 15 climbs from Crabble Road to the junction with London Road; this view was taken at the time of the opening of the route in 1905. (R.Hollingsbee Coll.)

20. Buckland Paper Mill is seen behind car 2
as it waits to pull away from Buckland towards
River. A covered top car is about to depart
from the depot spur in the direction of town.
(National Tramway Museum)

A person in a state of intoxication, or affected
with any infectious or contagious disease, shall not be
allowed to enter or mount upon any car, and if found in
or upon any car shall be immediately removed by or
under the direction of the conductor.

No person shall swear or use any obscene or offensive language whilst in or upon any car, or commit any
nuisance in or upon or against any car, or wilfully inter-
fere with the comfort of any passenger.

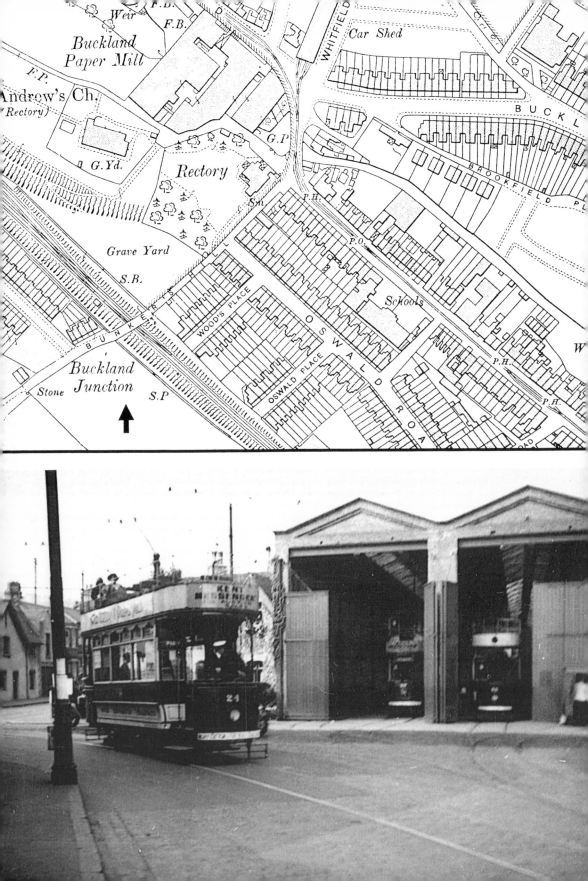

22. Seen outside Buckland Depot, the emerald green and cream livery of car 15 contrasts with the damp grey granite setts and the dull red brick walls of the paper mill. (National Tramway Museum)

21. At the extreme right of the picture can be glimpsed Mr.Oliver's Tea Bar which is parked in front of the depot doors on no.4 road, which was known amongst the staff as "rotten row." Old tramcars were parked on this depot track; Joe Harman remembers car 6 being brought out from mothballs for Cricket Week. Conducting on this veteran was a perilous experience due to the low handrails on the top deck. (National Tramway Museum. M.J.O'Connor)

23. The sun is out and a smart lady in a hat sits on the balcony of an equally smart cobalt blue and primrose liveried tramcar. The destination of car 20 is Sea Front, a location it would not have reached with its former owners, Birmingham Corporation!
(National Tramway Museum)

24. Buckland Depot was the setting for a number of official photos. Driver J.Larkins and conductress Amy Bean pose for the camera about 1919-20. (D.C.Padgham Coll.)

25. The conductor can just be seen collecting the fares on the top deck in this pre 1914 view. (C.Carter)

26. Depot road no.1 is empty, whilst cars 27 and 22 occupy roads 2 and 3 in this 1932 scene. Car 3 in dark red livery sweeps past. (National Tramway Museum. M.J.O'Connor)

27. A sight to gladen the hearts of any inhabitant of West Hartlepool who was taking a break in Dover in the summer of 1935. The three trams on view all hail from the north east coast and were transferred south to Kent in 1927. (National Tramway Museum. B.R.Miller)

28. It was said that the ex-Birmingham and Midland cars 11 and 12 were big, ungainly and cumbersome. Well, you can judge for yourself, as car 11 nudges forward on to the main line. (National Tramway Museum. M.J.O'Connor)

30. Dad holds his daughter up to watch car 23 which has just finished its run from town. A tram behind waits to pass in the opposite direction, whilst the smart gent in the bowler is no doubt enjoying the aroma of his pipe. (I.Gotheridge Coll.)

29. Buckland in 1936 and Joe Harman's lens catches car 21 passing the bus taking miners to a local pit. This area of Kent once had a rich coal seam and transport to the mines was taken over by East Kent buses in 1942. Buckland Depot also housed East Kent vehicles from 1942 to 1945 owing to the bombing of Dover Garage. (J.G.Harman)

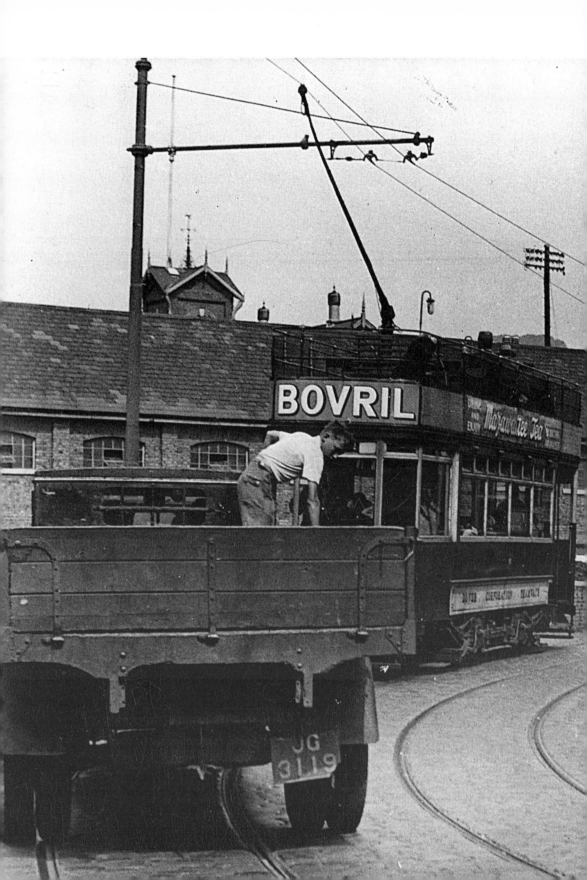

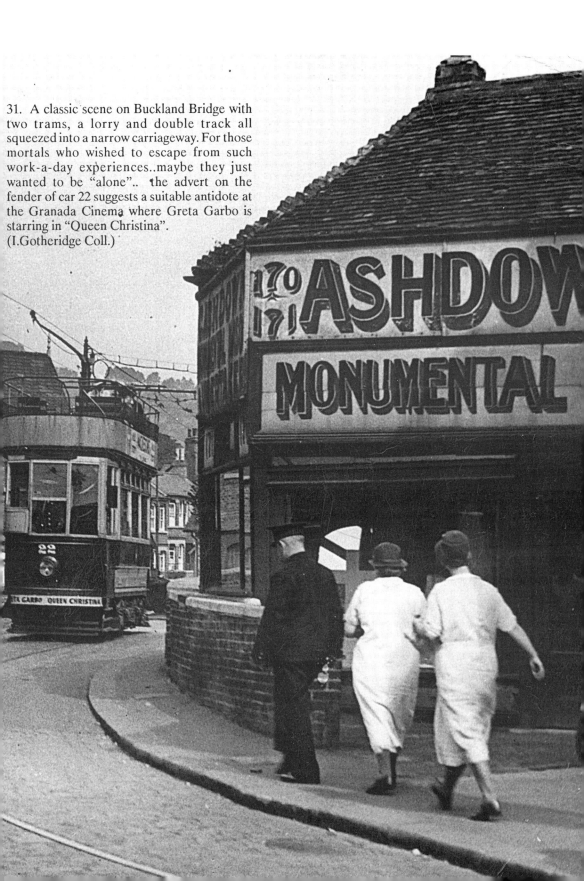

31. A classic scene on Buckland Bridge with two trams, a lorry and double track all squeezed into a narrow carriageway. For those mortals who wished to escape from such work-a-day experiences..maybe they just wanted to be "alone".. the advert on the fender of car 22 suggests a suitable antidote at the Granada Cinema where Greta Garbo is starring in "Queen Christina".
(I.Gotheridge Coll.)

32. A picture to enhance any chocolate box, only the hay wain has been replaced by an early Dover tram advertising Heinz 57 varieties! The River Dour flows sweetly on. (R.Hollingsbee Coll.)

33. A couple of trams pass on the bridge with car 24 very definite in its destination...Sea Front ONLY. (C.Carter)

34. The tram waits over the bridge and a fashionable group of young Dovorians is arrayed before the camera. (I.Gotheridge Coll.)

35. We leave Buckland Bridge with car 12 travelling proudly in the centre of the road; the boy running along the pavement may just beat it to the next stop. (I.Gotheridge Coll.)

36. Car 14 waits at the loop. It was here outside the Bull just before Buckland Bridge that young conductor Harman was struck by a motorcycle and sidecar as he was changing the points. Luckily he was uninjured, and the errant motorcyclist hurtling along London Road with visions of Brands Hatch in his head, was forced to stop. A cash offer of five shillings was accepted as immediate compensation. (National Tramway Museum. M.J.O'Connor)

37. On London Road by St.Radigunds Road, ex-Darlington car 8 makes a rare visit to the main line, normally these trams worked exclusively on the Maxton branch. (I.Gotheridge Coll.)

38. Lined up for the start of operations in 1897 by Cherry Tree Avenue, it will be noted that car 10 lacks a trolley pole and is, therefore, one of the two unpowered trailer cars. (Cassiers Magazine)

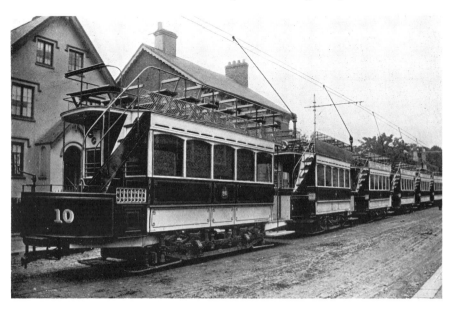

39. Dover High Street 1936 and the trams have barely a few more months to run. Already the increase in motor traffic is showing in the competition for road space. (J.G.Harman)

40. The electricity works was behind the Town Hall (see map on opposite page) and was operated by the Dover Electricity Supply Company until taken over by Dover Corporation in 1904. In 1921, the Tramways Department was being charged 4d per unit while other consumers were paying less than 2d. Dick, Kerr & Co Ltd supplied the generating equipment. (Cassiers Magazine)

41. Trams and clocks have played a seminal role in modern physics and the young Albert Einstein conceived the idea of relativity whilst commuting to work by tram. He speculated on what might happen if the tram accelerated away from a Town Hall clock at almost the speed of light; the answer, time slows down for those inside the tram. This theoretical work was done in Switzerland about the same time as car 17 passed Dover Town Hall, although its speed on this occasion was well below 300,000 kilometres per second! (R.J.Harley Coll.)

42. The overhead wires in Dover were originally positioned to one side of the road as shown in this view outside the Town Hall. Note the trolley pole of an approaching tram stretching to remain in contact with the power supply. The spacing of the wiring had to be altered when top covered cars arrived so that the trolley poles of passing trams did not collide. (R.J.Harley Coll.)

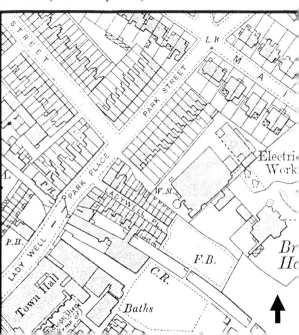

43. The threat to the tram's supremacy is very apparent in this photograph; the rivals vie with each other for control of the Dover streets. The headline on car 1's fender seems to say it all... "High Tension"   (I.Gotheridge Coll.)

44. St.Mary's Church in Biggin Street forms the background to this late Victorian scene. (R.J.Harley Coll.)

45. Two trams pass on market day and the carriers' baskets of local produce are piled high ready for the customers. It seems all human life is here at the Market Place in Dover around ninety years ago. (J.G.Harman Coll.)

46. Quieter times at the Market Place and car 9 crosses on its way to Buckland. (R.J.Harley Coll.)

47. Car 26 arrived in Dover in July 1920 and it is seen here in original condition. (J.G.Harman Coll.)

48. An unidentified tramcar pauses by one of the ornate centre standards in the Market Place. It is easy to forget what an amazing effect the powerful electric lights on the traction standard would have had on a population who were still living in the gaslight and candle age. (R.Hollingsbee Coll.)

49.   Another animated scene with car 15 passing the Garrick's Head pub which was demolished to make way for a branch of Lloyds Bank. The restaurant on the corner bears the well known Kentish name of Igglesden. (R.J.Harley Coll.)

50.   A fine broadside shot of tramcar and passengers all eager to participate in this new wonder of the transport world. After the photographer had finished how about taking up the offer of an Ahdeekho Tea or a Brussels Coffee? (National Tramway Museum)

51.   Car 2 heads along King Street past the General Post Office. The centre poles remained in use throughout the life of the tramways. (R.J.Harley Coll.)

52. The constable in the picture is following car 9 in Bench Street and was probably thinking in terms of "as I proceeded in a northerly direction." One wonders whether the gentleman on the top deck with his arm out was gesticulating at the bystander. (R.J.Harley Coll.)

54. On the corner of Northampton Street and Bench Street a tram waits in the sunshine. (National Tramway Museum)

53. In the days before the information technology era when travel information for the public came in a more basic form, a notice above the clock on the traction standard indicates Next Car For River. The service interval on the main line to Buckland was 7 minutes and to River 21 minutes, with the round trip from Pier to River taking 63 minutes. (C.Carter)

55. A few moments later than the previous
photo and a covered top car in dark red livery
pulls up. (National Tramway Museum)

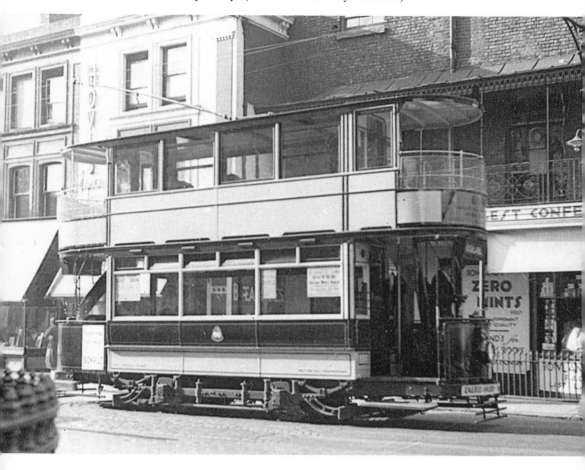

A person whose dress or clothing might, in the
opinion of the conductor of a car, soil or injure the seats,
linings or cushions of the carriage, or the dress or clothing of any passenger, or a person who, in the opinion of
the conductor, might for any other reason be offensive to
passengers, shall not be entitled to enter or remain in or
upon any car, and may be prevented from entering or remaining in or upon any car, and shall not enter, or be or
remain in or upon any part thereof, after having been
requested not to do so by the conductor, and, if found in
or upon any car, shall, on request of the conductor, leave
the car upon the fare, if previously paid, being returned.

56. Snargate Street is shown here in the first
decade of the twentieth century.
(I.Gotheridge Coll.)

57. Car 26 in emerald green livery pauses at
Snargate Street loop. The photographer is
standing on the south side where shops and
houses once existed. Note the drop windows
on the top deck; it must have been a warm day.
(G.N.Southerden)

58. This is a fine panorama of seafront Dover. In the distance a tram wends its way along Snargate Street, whilst in the foreground another car enters Strond Street in the direction of the Harbour Station. Note the standard gauge railway tracks used for traffic from the Prince of Wales Pier. Rebuilding Snargate Street seems to have become a local obsession, and at the time of writing (1993) it was being altered yet again.
(National Tramway Museum)

59. Taken from the front balcony of the tram waiting at the loop, we see a car coming from Strond Street about to cross the railway at George Corner. The date is 1934 and the tramways were living on borrowed time. (G.N.Southerden)

60. A line of Southern Railway goods wagons blocks the street, leaving just enough room for car 3 to set down a passenger. Large quantities of East Kent coal were exported from the Eastern Arm. (I.Gotheridge Coll.)

61. Car 22 has just cleared the railway crossing; duplication of tracks was necessary due to differences in gauge and wheel profile. (G.N.Southerden)

62. A classic encounter on Strond Street. The ex-SECR P class 0-6-0 tank locomotive is working stock to the Harbour Station. Car 27 scurries by on the wrong side of the road, but then who worried about such niceties in those days! (G.N.Southerden)

The Harbour Tramway is illustrated in the Middleton Press album *Faversham to Dover*.

PIER WARD

T.Cu

TRAMWAY

Chy.

S.Ps.

Hotels

UNION STREET

Wellington
Bridge

QUAY

Cn.   F.W.

Lock

Esp

Holy Trinity Ch.

L.B

CUSTOM HOUSE QUAY

GRANVILLE
BASIN

Cn.

Cn.

TIDA
HARBO

Vic.

L.B

P.H.

P.H.

P.H.

STROND STREET

P.H.

P.H.

Mooring Posts

F.W. S.

Granville Bridge

Lock

WALL

CROSS

F.W.

Dolphin Je

Harbour Station

Drainage
Works

STROND LANE

OXENDEN

WATER LN.

ELIZABETH

STREET

P.H.

Custom
House

Cn.

Inn

Nort

School

S.B.

P.H.

Hotel

Cr.

HAWKESBURY ST.

STREET

P.H.

PARADISE ST.

TOWER LANE

ROUND TOWER ST.

S.B.

P.H.

S.P

Cr.   H.W.M.O.T.

BULWARK

STREET

P.H.

YOUNG TOWER ST.

Inn
P.H.

Hotel

Hotel

S.P.

Inn

CLARENCE PLACE

Hotels

P.H
P.H

84

GREAT ST.

46
56

Engine
House

COUNCIL HOUSE STREET

Ch

MIDDLE ROW

SEVEN ST.

P.H

Hotel

L.B

B.S.

F.W.

BEACH STREET

P.H.

P.H.

S.Ps

S.P

S.P.

S.B.

S.B. Cr.   Cr.

Town Station

S.P

63. The track seen here was doubled in 1904. Note the side mounted trolley standard on this tram as it passes Hawkesbury Street Junction signal box. (National Tramway Museum)

64. With the end of the line in sight, car 17 halts for the photographer. In the background the Western Heights dominate the town. (J.G.Harman)

65. The full spectacle of the opening ceremony in 1897 is captured on film as the inaugural procession lines up to proceed along Strond Street. The barrow with the baskets belongs to Scott's the Dyers of Snargate Street. (R.Hollingsbee Coll.)

66. One of the 1898 cars stands at the terminus after the route had been cut back from Clarence Place. (C.Carter)

67. George Gundry was on hand to record car 16 standing on the single track curve which led originally over the level crossing towards the final passing loop in Clarence Place. The date is 1922. (G.L.Gundry)

68. In 1926 the terminal arrangement was altered when the Southern Railway built a concrete footbridge to replace the level crossing. The curved tram track was removed and we see here car 3 standing on the single track terminus stub. (J.G.Harman)

69. Activity at Pier terminus. Double ended tramcars could reverse with the minimum of fuss, the driver went to the opposite end of the tram, the conductor turned the trolley, passengers boarded and then you were off. It is a pity that G.N.Southerden who took this shot, did not have access to colour film in 1934. What a splendid contrast this would have been between dark red car 27 and dark blue car 22, and of course in those days of yore public service vehicles were regularly cleaned! (G.N.Southerden)

70. The solid structure of car 11 rests before the return trip to Buckland. Each driver had a key which he inserted into the Bundy time clock seen on the pavement to the right of the tram. This recorded the time of departure. (G.N.Southerden)

71. The harbour, the quayside, the steamers, the cranes and car 5 fit together well in this 1932 view. A stylish street lamp stands next to a couple who are looking wistfully across the water. (National Tramway Museum. M.J.O'Connor)

72. The sun is obviously too much for at least one intending passenger; the motorman waits in the shade of car 26. On days like these it was pleasantly cool on the driver's platform, but come winter, the task must have been very uncomfortable. (National Tramway Museum)

→

73. The weather is colder and the mist rolls in from the sea as Conductor Harman has stationed himself on the top deck to take this photo of car 20 about to leave Pier terminus. Also evident is the SR's new footbridge. (J.G.Harman)

→

74. Our intrepid conductor, not satisfied with all the normal angles for photography, has climbed up to the roof of a nearby hotel at Crosswall to get this shot of car 22. The footbridge was associated with other railway alterations which included closure of Harbour Station in 1927. (J.G.Harman)

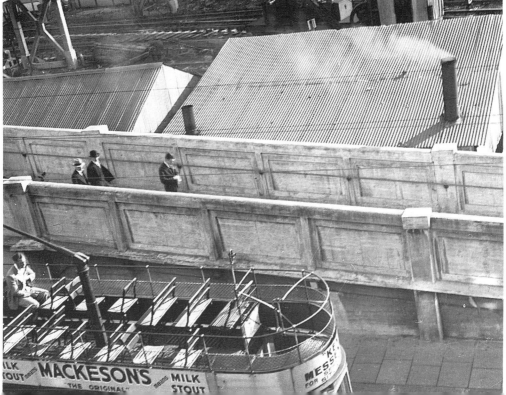

75. Continuing the aerial theme, Joe Harman snapped the "trouble cart" early one Sunday morning; this horse drawn tower wagon was usually kept on "rotten row" in Buckland Depot. Here we see Messrs Knott and Creed debating which bit of the overhead to fix next. When the two gentlemen were shown this photo, Joe was loudly berated for missing out the horse which was standing patiently off camera. (J.G.Harman)

⟶

77. Joe Harman's quick turn in reponse to his name being called has been captured for posterity. I hope he did check that the trolley was on the wire before attempting to set off. The tower was part of Harbour Station. (J.G.Harman)

76. There weren't that many tramway photographers in the 1930s and those who got to Dover seemed to have made a bee- line for Pier terminus. The two smiling girls on the top deck front seat lend a very human quality to this view. (National Tramway Museum. R.Neate)

DOVER CORPORATION TRAMWAYS.

PRIVATE. MOTORMEN AND CONDUCTORS' DUTY LIST. *From 18th Oct., 1926.*

Duty No.	Report.	To work.	Relieved.		Off Duty.	Remarks.
MAIN LINE.			From	To		
,, 1	5.20 a.m.	5.28 a.m.	6.49 a.m.	8. 0 a.m.	12.57 p.m.	
,, 2	5.40 a.m.	5.47 a.m.	7.53 a.m.	9.17 a.m.	2. 6 p.m.	
,, 3	5.20 a.m.	6.45 a.m.	9. 9 a.m.	11. 2 a.m.	2.27 p.m.	
,, 4	7.26 a.m.	7.34 a.m.	11. 0 a.m. 1.32 p.m	11.56 a.m. 3.24 p.m.	6.10 p.m.	
,, 5	12.22 p.m.	12.31 p.m.	3.22 p.m.	4.55 p.m.	10.50 p.m.	
,, 6	2. 0 p.m.	2. 8 p.m.	4.53 p.m.	6.12 p.m.	10.40 p.m.	
,, 7	2.20 p.m.	2.28 p.m.	6.38 p.m.	7.15 p.m.	11. 0 p.m.	
,, 8	12 50 p.m.	12.59 p.m.	5.22 p.m.	6.40 p.m.	10.10 p.m.	
,, 9	7.30 a.m.	7.39 a.m.	12.29 p.m.	4.27 p.m.	7.13 p.m.	
Odds	6.50 a.m.	7. 5 a.m.	9.16 a.m. 12. 0 p.m.	10.16 a.m. 1.30 p.m.	5.19 p.m.	Work to Inspector's Instructions.
RIVER.						
,, A	7.15 a.m.	7.25 a.m.	11.35 a.m.	11.50 a.m.	1.12 p.m.	
,, B	7.40 a.m.	7.46 a.m.	11.56 a.m	1.33 p.m.	6. 4 p.m.	
,, C	1. 5 p.m.	1.13 p.m.	5. 0 p.m.	6. 5 p.m.	10.49 p.m.	
,, D	1. 5 p.m.	1.12 p.m.	4.40 p.m.	5.22 p.m.	10.30 p.m.	
,, E	9. 0 a.m.	9.10 a.m.	1.18 p.m.	5. 0 p.m.	8.30 p.m.	
MAXTON LINE. 1	5.20 a.m.	5.28 a.m.	7.25 a.m.	8.36 a.m.	1. 5 p.m.	
,, 2	6.35 a.m.	6.45 a.m.	8.34 a.m.	12.17 p.m.	5.50 p.m.	
,, 3	7.20 a.m.	7.28 a.m.	12.16 p.m.	4.20 p.m.	8.31 p.m.	
,, 4	1. 0 p.m.	1. 6 p.m.	4.12 p.m.	5.51 p.m.	11. 0 p.m.	
,, 5	12.25 p.m.	12.31 p.m.	4.19 p.m.	6.19 p.m.	10.50 p.m.	
,, 6	7.30 a.m	7.39 a.m.	12.30 p.m.	4.13 p.m.	6.18 p.m.	

SPECIAL NOTES.—In order to keep themselves familiar with the ready use of the Emergency Brake, Drivers must as the opportunity occurs, occasionally use this brake and should always test it when taking over a car.

It is very necessary that Duty Men taking cars from shed shall turn up strictly at the times shown in above Duty List, also the various reliefs are taken up sharp at time, otherwise it is impossible for "Off Duty" Men to get away as arranged.

Changing over duties is strictly prohibited, unless official permission is obtained. Each duty is to be completed as shown above.

Sunday is to be counted in reckoning duty numbers.

IMPORTANT.—When bringing Cars from Buckland Depot, Conductors must give a good look out and Drivers drive **very cautiously** owing to Main Road Crossing immediately across front of Shed and to the frequency of passing vehicles.

ERNEST H. BOND, *General Manager.*

78. The indicator blind is being turned from Pier to River on car 4. Only open top trams were allowed beyond Buckland; an encounter with the low railway bridge over Crabble Lane would have caused an embarrassing accident for any top covered car. (National Tramway Museum. J.Chettleburgh)

79. Looking very smart in his summer uniform, motorman Cyril Deverson poses in front of his tram in the summer of 1935. (National Tramway Museum. B.R.Miller)

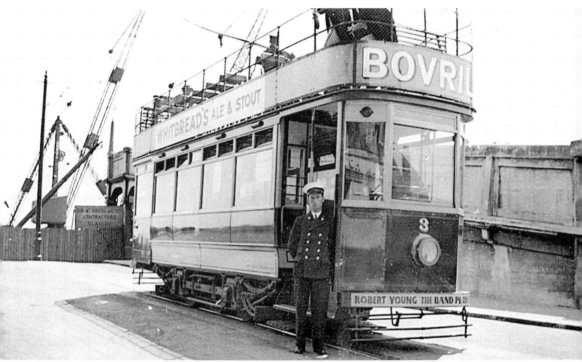

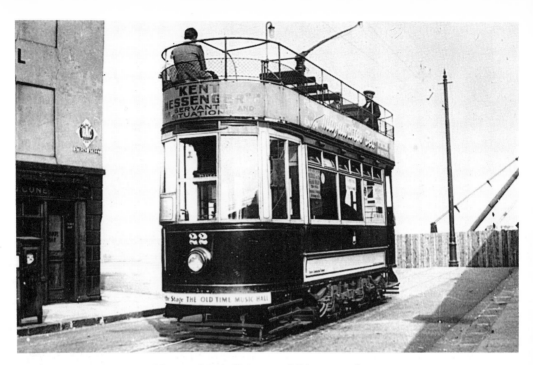

80. A last glimpse of Pier terminus as
ex-Birmingham car 22 waits to depart.
(G.N.Southerden)

2. Maxton Branch

82. Worthington Street is the setting for the start of our excursion along the Folkestone Road route. Car 21 waits opposite the ornate shelter awning fixed to the front of Timothy Whites. (G.N.Southerden)

81. The line in Clarence Place was short lived, closing in April 1898. The tram service was cut back to Crosswall because of delays caused by the closing of the level crossing gates seen in the background. Car 10, a former trailer newly motorised, has made it across the railway and halts amongst the porters with their boxes of fish. The nearby Town Station closed in 1914. (I.Gotheridge Coll.)

83. A joyful occasion as we witness the bride arriving by tramcar for her wedding at Christ Church on 19th April 1901. The guests are huddled in the lower saloon waiting to get off. No doubt some of them cherished hopes that the reception would live up to the groom's surname, Mr A.E.Binge. (J.G.Harman Coll.)

84. A tranquil 1898 scene on the Folkestone Road; car 7 hums steadily past some interested pedestrians. (J.G.Harman Coll.)

85. The Maxton branch was the home of the ex-Darlington cars which shuttled up and down many times a day; car 9 has just crossed the railway bridge at Priory Station. Arriving train passengers were greeted by a notice, "Take The Tram To The Seafront." Unfortunately there was no through service, thus obliging holidaymakers and locals alike to change at Worthington Street to a Main Line tram. (I.Gotheridge Coll.)

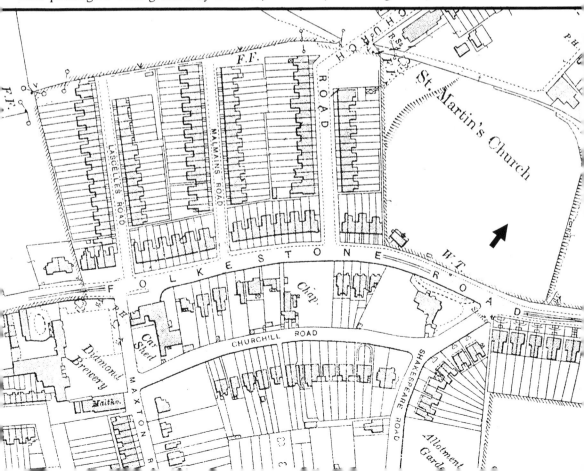

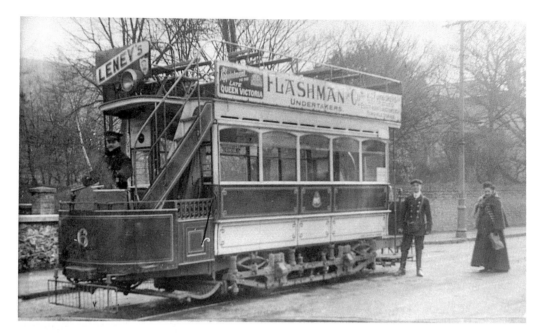

86. The terminus at Maxton and driver F.Hilt
turns to the camera. Conductor and lady passenger also take part in this posed scene.
(J.G.Harman Coll.)

87. The depot at Maxton on 31st December
1936, the last day of trams in Dover. We can
only guess what was going through the minds
of the two crew members. (J.G.Harman)

88. Every tramway undertaking had to rely on a loyal staff to cope with the technical side of operation. A group of craftsmen surrounds car 3 which has been rebuilt at Maxton Depot. (J.G.Harman Coll.)

89. Maxton Depot supplied the trams for the Folkestone Road and two of its tramway inhabitants are pictured being made ready for service. (G.N.Southerden)

90. These two trams at Maxton were equipped with outside springs on the trolley standards. There was at least one incident of a top deck passenger getting his fingers trapped and suffering an enforced ride to the end of the line. (I.Gotheridge Coll.)

91. A splendid view of one of the ex-Birmingham Corporation cars at Maxton terminus. The depot building was demolished in 1993. (G.N.Southerden)

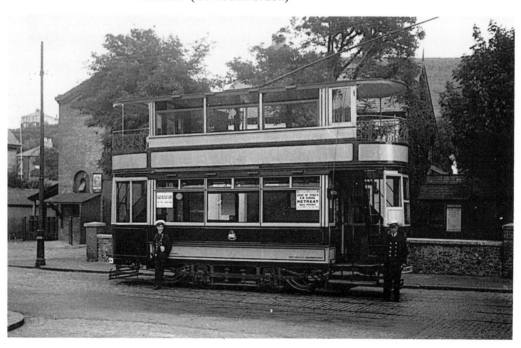

92. Car 8 is pictured here in its first Dover livery of emerald green and cream. The sign is for the Orange Tree pub which was adjacent to the depot. (National Tramway Museum. M.J.O'Connor)

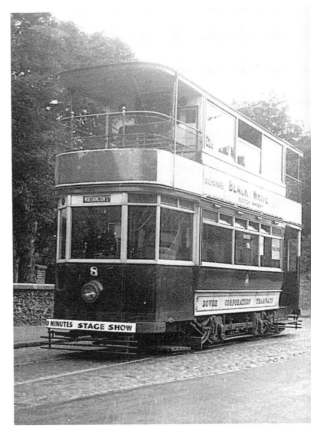

93. Two years on from the previous photo and car 8 is now painted dark red and ivory and the indicator box has been removed from the top deck to a position just above the driver. (G.N.Southerden)

No dog or other animal shall be allowed in the interior of any car nor in any case in which the conveyance of such dog or other animal is offensive or an annoyance to any passenger shall the same be allowed on the outside of any car. No person shall take a dog or other animal into or upon any car after having been requested not to do so by the conductor or any passenger. Any dog or other animal taken into or on any car in breach of this Regulation shall be removed by the person in charge of such dog or other animal from the car immediately upon request by the conductor, and in default of compliance with such request may be removed by or under the direction of the conductor.

94. "All I seek, the heaven above and the road below me." These lines from "Songs of Travel" by Robert Louis Stevenson were set to music by Ralph Vaughan Williams, inspired it is said by a walk on the Downs seen here in this partly restored picture. The date is about 1900 and with the sentiments of R.L.Stevenson in mind we conclude our nostalgic journey over the Dover Tramways. (J.G.Harman Coll.)

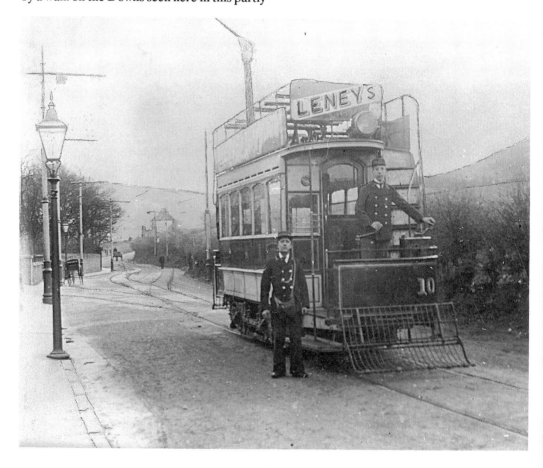

3. Rolling Stock

ROLLING STOCK PURCHASED NEW BY DOVER CORPORATION

CARS 1-10. Built by Brush at Loughborough in 1897. Cars 3 and 10 were supplied as unpowered trailers and all cars were equipped with 6ft. wheelbase Peckham Cantilever trucks. The trailers were motorised and most of this group were withdrawn in the 1920s.

CARS 11-14. Built by George Milnes & Co. at Birkenhead in 1898. Generally similar in body design to the earlier batch, car 12 was fitted with an experimental top cover in 1904 and car 13 was rebuilt in 1926 and lasted until 1936. Cars 11, 12 and 14 were scrapped in 1927.

CARS 15-16. Built by J.G.Brill at Philadelphia in 1898. The final two cars built to the original short canopy design, they were both rebuilt in 1927 and car 16 was given a windscreen. They were little used after the late 1920s, but they survived till the end. They had 6ft. Brill 21E trucks.

CAR 17. Built at Preston in 1902, this was a typical British reversed staircase four wheel tram of the period. The staircase was altered to the normal version in 1918 and the car which had a 6ft. Brill 21E truck, was disposed of in 1930.

CARS 18-21. Built at Preston in 1905 on 6ft. wheelbase 21E trucks, these were traditional open top trams. Car 20 was involved in the Crabble accident, was rebuilt and finally scrapped in 1926. Cars 18, 19 and 21 survived until 1933.

CARS 22-24. Built by Brush at Loughborough in 1912, these cars were supplied on the slightly longer 6ft. 6ins. truck. They were solidly constructed and car 22 was scrapped in 1933 but its motors lasted until 1936.

CARS 25-27. Built at Preston in 1920 to what was then an antiquated design. One can only assume that the Corporation wanted to stick to a type of car that was "tried and tested" rather than invest in a more modern tram. All of these cars were fitted with second hand top covers from the Birmingham and Midland Joint Committee Tramways. They were repainted dark red and ivory before they reached the end of the line in 1936. They had English Electric Preston trucks of 7ft. 6ins. wheelbase.

ROLLING STOCK PURCHASED SECOND HAND FROM OTHER OPERATORS

CARS 1-5. Built at Preston in 1913 for West Hartlepool and acquired by Dover in 1927. These were four wheel open top cars with windscreens and, unusually for the era, transverse seating on the lower deck. Car 2 appeared in Dover emerald green and ivory livery, but the stair stringers remained dark red. The rest stayed in their original dark red colours and this scheme became the standard for Dover. They ran on 8ft. wheelbase trucks.

CARS 8-9. Built at Preston in 1913 for Darlington Corporation and acquired by Dover in 1926. Both cars were top covered with windscreens; they had 8ft. wheelbase trucks. They appeared in Dover wearing the emerald green livery, but were subsequently repainted dark red.

CARS 11-12. Built at Tividale Works in 1915 for the Birmingham and Midland Tramways, they arrived in Dover in 1928. They were tall, solid cars running on 8ft. 6ins. trucks, and they were equipped with partial windscreens. Both were repainted emerald green.

CARS 6, 7, 10, 14 and 17. These trams were from the Tividale "stable" and differed from the previous Birmingham and Midland acquisitions in not possessing windscreens. Car 14 was built at Tividale, but the rest were built originally by Brush in 1904. They were painted dark red and ivory, and were acquired in 1930.

CARS 19-22. Built at Preston in 1905 for Birmingham Corporation, they were bought by Dover in 1933. Cars 19 and 20 used 6ft. 6ins. trucks, however, cars 21 and 22 retained their 6ft. wheelbase Brill 21E trucks. Car 22 was converted back to open top condition for use on the River service. They kept their Birmingham cobalt blue and primrose livery.

95. Car 2 hauls trailer car 3 past Pencester Road. Note the original condition of these cars without decency boards along the top deck. The original Dover livery was medium green and ivory. (Street Railway Journal. USA)

96. Driver J. Taylor perished with thousands of his compatriots on the Somme in 1916. Here we see him in charge of car 4 which was beginning to show its age. (D.C. Padgham Coll.)

97. This picture of car 16 was taken around 1920; note the double doors to the lower saloon. The fleet number and title of the undertaking were in gold letters shaded red. (D.C. Padgham Coll.)

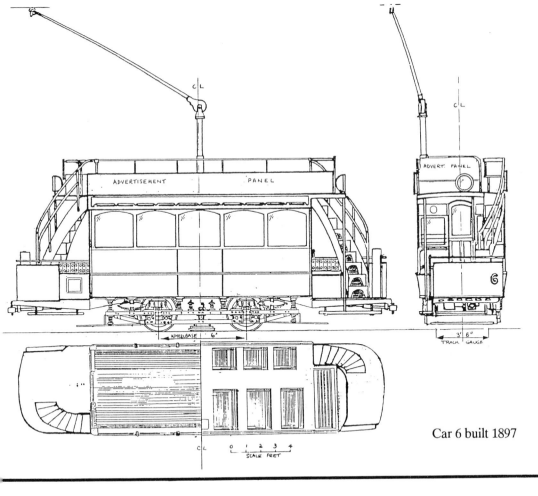

ADVERTISEMENT PANEL

WHEELBASE 6'

ADVERT PANEL

ADVERT PANEL

3' 6"
TRACK GAUGE

0 1 2 3 4
SCALE FEET

Car 6 built 1897

98. Taken for publicity purposes, car 16 sports an early type of lifeguard which resembled a folding bed without the mattress. The brown and cream advert for Leney's Ales was a common one on Dover trams; the firm was taken over by Fremlins in 1926.
(National Tramway Museum)

99. Car 16 in its rebuilt form shows what could be done to modernise the original design and provide more protection for the motorman against the elements. Stickers were placed on the car fenders for the latest events at the Granada Cinema which opened in 1930. (R.Elliott)

101. At Buckland Depot we can see the differing platform and staircase styles of cars 20 and 2. (R.J.Harley Coll.)

100. Snapped in 1922, car 13 looks very antiquated. Four years later this car was rebuilt and it saw out the remaining time of the system. (G.L.Gundry)

102. Car 18, a typical British tram of 1905, seen here in August 1919. Note the wire and metal lifeguards. (D.C.Padgham Coll.)

103. Car 21 outside Buckland Depot in 1921. The poster on the lower saloon window details the Christmas matches to be played by Dover United. (J.G.Harman Coll.)

104. Car 23 is shown in its last form at River
terminus. (J.G.Harman)

105. Car 26 was delivered in 1920 in the new,
brighter emerald green and ivory colours.
(I.Gotheridge Coll.)

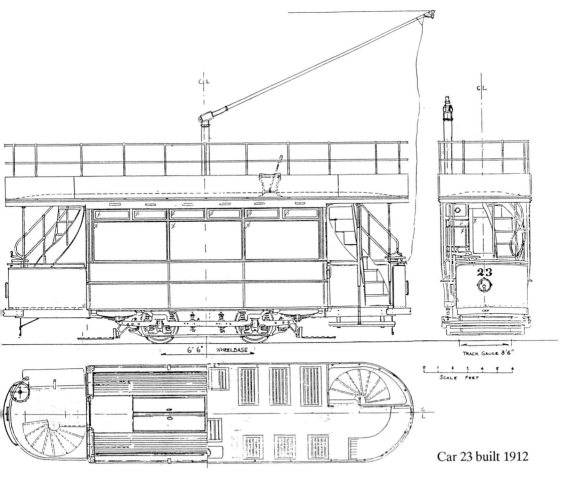

Car 23 built 1912

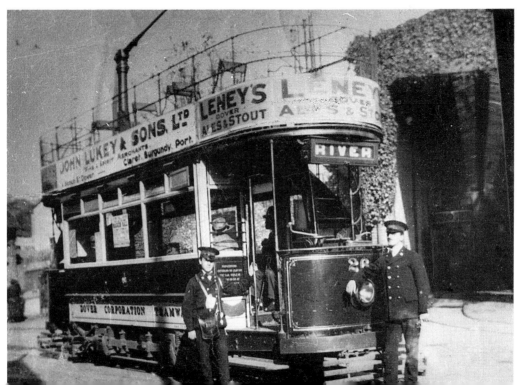

Car 26 (top covered version)

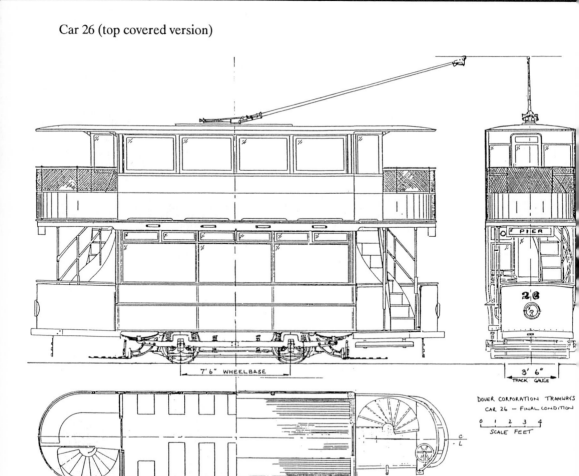

PIER

2 6

DOVER CORPORATION TRAMWAYS
CAR 26 — FINAL CONDITION

7' 6" WHEELBASE

3' 6"
TRACK GAUGE

0 1 2 3 4
SCALE FEET

106. Pictured at almost the same spot as the previous photo, car 26 has had a top cover added, thereby precluding its use on the River service. Note the odd window arrangement, four main windows on the top deck plus one wing window opposite the stairwell. The lower deck retained its three window saloon.
(National Tramway Museum. M.J.O'Connor)

107. The transverse lower deck seats on ex-West Hartlepool car 4 can clearly be seen. The dark red livery on these trams weathered to a chocolate brown colour. This view dates from December 1934; note the message on the dash urging caution on passing motorists. (D.C.Padgham Coll.)

108. The ex-West Hartlepool trams were handsome cars and their clean lines show up in this photo taken at Crosswall terminus. (National Tramway Museum. J.Chettleburgh)

109. A fine end view showing many of the minor details sought by tramway modellers. Car 5 is standing at Crosswall early in 1936. Note the blue Hawksfield Coals advert. (J.G.Harman)

110. George Attwood and George Smith crew ex-Birmingham and Midland car 7. Climbing that narrow, twisting staircase could not have been easy for the elderly or infirm. (J.G.Harman)

→

112. Car 10 was a solidly built tramcar. Here we see the ex- Birmingham and Midland tram at Worthington Street terminus in 1932. (National Tranway Museum. M.J.O'Connor)

111. Ex-Darlington car 9 at Maxton terminus in 1932 shortly after its repaint in dark red. (National Tramway Museum. M.J.O'Connor)

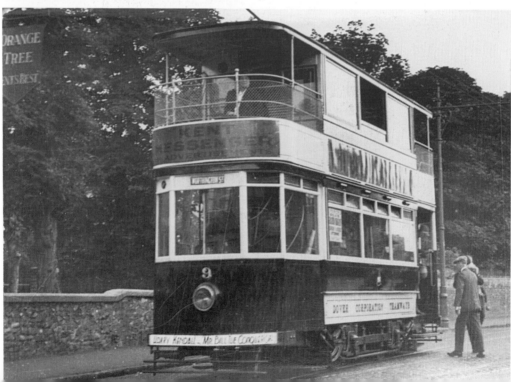

The conductor of each car shall enforce these Bye-Laws and Regulations, and prevent any breach thereof to the best of his ability.

Any person offending against or committing a breach of any of these Bye-Laws or Regulations shall be liable to a penalty of Forty Shillings; provided nevertheless that the Justices or Court before whom any complaint may be made, or any proceedings may be taken in respect of any such offence, may, if they think fit, adjudge the payment as a penalty of any sum less than the full amount of the penalty imposed by these Bye-Laws and Regulations.

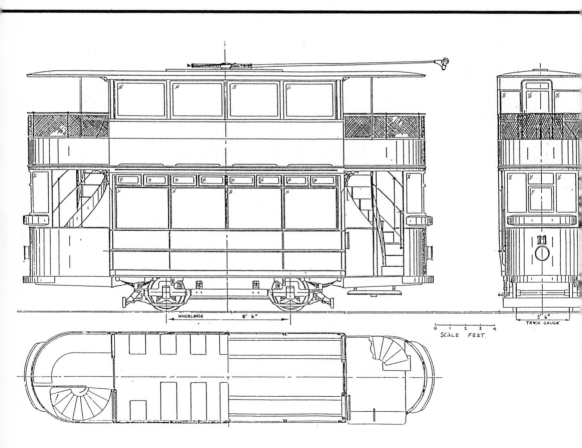

Car 11 (ex Birmingham & Midland)
acquired 1928

113. Car 11 was another Tividale product, it differed from its sister car 12 in not having a wing window on the upper deck. (National Tramway Museum. M.J.O'Connor)

A passenger not being an artizan, mechanic, or daily labourer, within the true intent and meaning of the Dover Corporation Tramways Order, 1896, shall not use or attempt to use any Ticket intended only for such artizans, mechanics, or daily labourers.

Personal luggage not exceeding 28 lbs. in weight (including the tools of artizans, mechanics, and daily labourers) may be carried by hand or, unless otherwise permitted by the conductor, shall be placed on the front or driver's platform. The conductor may decline to take into or upon the car any luggage of a form or description to annoy or inconvenience any passenger.

Car 19 (ex Birmingham Corporation)
acquired 1933

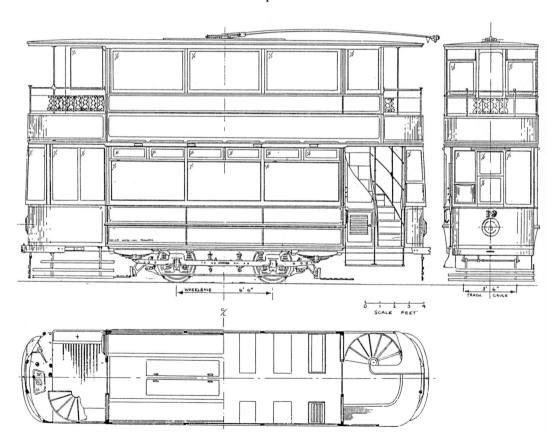

114. Worthington Street in 1934 and ex-
Birmingham Corporation car 19 waits in the
sunshine. Note that this car has lost its wing
mirror from the front windscreen.
(G.N.Southerden)

115. Car 22 was a cut down Birmingham car; the top deck fittings came from a scrapped Dover car. The trolley standard was painted green and the original blue livery had weathered to almost black. (G.N.Southerden)

117. The "Tramway And Railway World" used this illustration in their issue of 10th January 1907. It shows a grinding machine and rail shaper in operation on Folkestone Road near Priory Station. Note the long pole attached to the overhead to draw power for the machinery. In the background is a very rare view of car 14 with its experimental top cover.
(Tramway And Railway World)

116. The Dover trams are represented in miniature on the 1:16 scale layout constructed by Ron Leach which now resides at Dover Transport Museum. (R.J.Harley)

118. A sight to bring tears to all those, like the staff at the National Tramway Museum in Crich, Derbyshire, who engage in restoration work. The trams are being smashed up! Such a scene greeted Joe Harman and his camera at Buckland Depot in 1937. Some of the maintenance pits have already been filled in and the top covers are being detached violently from the lower decks. (J.G.Harman)

119. In the still, clear winter air of January 1937 the last of the Dover trams await their fate. No more would they rock and sway along the town's streets and over grass grown tracks past hedgerows to River. Their time had passed. Sic Transit Gloria Mundi. (J.G.Harman)

120. The official seals of Dover were carried on the waist panels of all tramcars.

VILLE · ET · PORTUS · DOVER

DOVER.